Seeing Jesus

Exploring the Bible through contemporary art

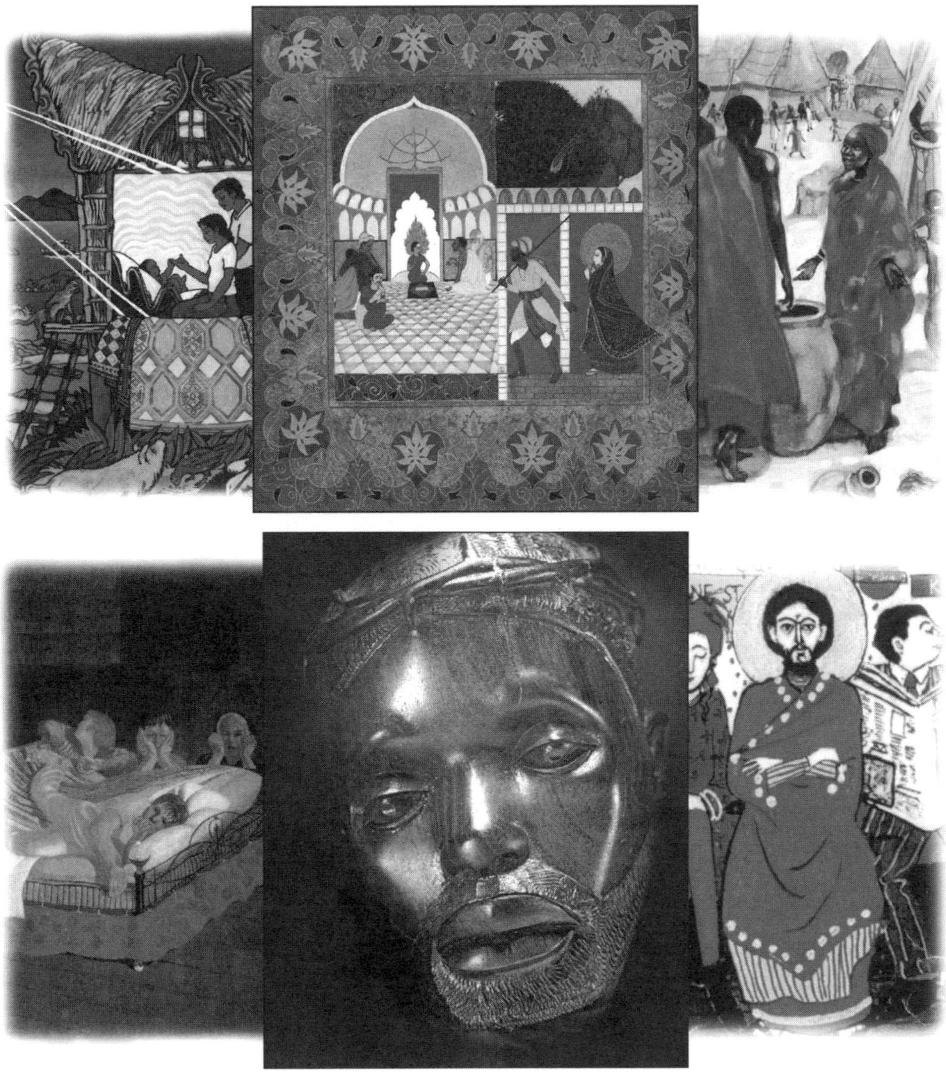

Resources for Bible study and house groups by Nicola Slee

CHRISTIAN
education

Written by: Nicola Slee

Nicola Slee is a freelance writer and educator based at The Queen's Foundation, Birmingham.
This material has been developed from discussions by an ecumenical group consisting of: Anne Dunkley (Baptist), Judy Jarvis (Methodist), Tony McCaffrey (Roman Catholic), Stuart Scott (United Reformed Church) and Elizabeth Bruce Whitehorn (Christian Education).

Other Bible study guides written by Nicola Slee and published by Christian Education Publications: *Remembering Mary*, *Searching Stories*, *Songs of Life*, *Prisons and Palaces*.

Published by:
Christian Education Publications
1020 Bristol Road
Selly Oak
Birmingham
B29 6LB

British Cataloguing-in-Publication Data:
A catalogue record is available for this book from the British Library.

ISBN 0-904024-65-3

First published 2005

Designed and typeset by: Christian Education Publications

Printed and bound by: Stephen Austin & Sons Limited

CONTENTS

INTRODUCTION

The nature and aims of the material

The main purpose of *Seeing Jesus* is to encourage adults, either on their own or in a group setting, to engage with the Christian gospel in new and stimulating ways, through a study of selected visual representations of Jesus and related biblical passages. Six highly original images of Jesus have been chosen to pinpoint different stages of Jesus' life – from his birth and boyhood, through his ministry of teaching and healing to his death and resurrection.

The pictures also represent different artists' impressions of Jesus from different cultures and settings in the modern world. They offer very different theological interpretations of who Jesus is and what he means to different groups of people in different places, challenging viewers to consider afresh the relevance of the Jesus story to their own settings and lives.

Each study is intended to engage three distinct but related stories or contexts: first, the story told by the picture itself, to which you are invited to give your primary attention; second, the text of the Bible, in a passage or passages chosen to illuminate the picture; and third, the context of your own life, setting and concerns, to which the picture and the biblical texts can speak. As each individual or group brings their own questions, concerns, needs and experiences to the visual representations of Christ and the biblical passages, new insights may be gained and new awareness given of the meaning of Jesus and his liberating gospel to our world.

Doing theology with the eyes

We live in a highly visual world, in which we are daily bombarded and saturated by images from the media – cinema and television, mobile phones and computers, advertising hoardings, newspapers and magazines spew out visual images and messages constantly. Yet most of these images are ephemeral, passing across our vision for a fleeting moment or two before they are gone, replaced by the next. Little in our culture encourages us to look attentively or deeply, to pay close attention to images of enduring worth, to *contemplate* with the eye.

Religious traditions have long recognised the power of the pictorial to teach, to inspire, to transmit the faith, to communicate the essence and the power of religion in ways that go beyond words. Before the advent of the book and long after it, believers of every tradition have been instructed in the faith by picture, colour and shape as much as by precept, law or verbal instruction. You have only to walk into a medieval cathedral or a mosque to experience the power of a great building to communicate faith. Long before people could read the scriptures, they could 'read' stained glass windows which depicted biblical stories in vivid technicolour, or meditate upon the beauty and splendour of Allah through the intricate patterns of floor tile and calligraphy.

Since the Reformation, the Protestant church has tended to be highly suspicious of the visual and other arts, prioritising the word above every other form of expression and rejecting the possibility that God might be known and encountered through the pictorial, the dramatic, the musical, the sensuous. One of the great fruits of the modern ecumenical movement has been a new openness in Protestant traditions to symbol, sacrament and the senses as avenues through which God can speak and work in the world – something that the Roman Catholic and Orthodox traditions never forgot, with their strong emphasis on sacraments and the symbolic. Christians are rediscovering the richness and beauty of the arts and the human senses, recognising that Christ the Word became flesh and continues to be incarnated among us in living colour, sound, pattern and shape, in the stuff of human flesh and lives.

In these studies, you are invited to do theology, to approach prayer, to encounter Christ and your neighbour, not first and foremost in abstraction or analytical thought, but with the *eye*, in and through the senses and the imagination. You are invited to meet God in colour and texture, shape and pattern, concrete detail and story, striking image and symbol. The aim is to see with the heart and the mind, to recognise and encounter Christ afresh.

For some individuals, this kind of approach to Bible study through the visual arts will be naturally appealing, stimulating and exciting. Many adults already have a keen love of the arts; perhaps they paint or draw themselves or simply enjoy looking at paintings, whether they have received any formal art education or not. But for others this approach may be new, unusual, difficult and even threatening. They are not used to looking at paintings and have never been taught how to find meaning in visual art. They find much contemporary art alienating, ugly, random or dull. Art is for others, not for them. It leaves them cold, or embarrassed, or feeling inadequate.

Learning to look

For all of us, there is a need to *learn* to look. There is a discipline of learning to 'read' paintings, in the same way as we have to learn how to read a book for meaning. It is something that comes with practice, and it is also something that can be immensely enriched by sharing the process with other learners. One of the great delights of looking at paintings or sculpture in a group setting is that other people always see something different from what *I* see, ask different questions, bring other insights – and that can open up as well as challenge my own reaction to the work of art. No one person is the 'expert', all have something to contribute. Even the artist himself or herself never has the monopoly of meaning: others will see 'more' or other things than the artist intended. Individuals who might struggle to find meaning in a painting on their own can be encouraged in a group to learn to see through the insights of others.

Annie Dillard, a Pulitzer-winning writer with an eye for the extraordinary in the ordinary, writes about two different kinds of seeing, and you will need to employ both kinds as you approach the paintings and sculpture in this study. First, there is the kind of seeing that is analysing and probing, a kind of seeing that involves the active co-operation of brain and eye, where we notice every detail of a face or a room, subjecting things to minute scrutiny and asking questions of what is there, leaving nothing to casual glance or lazy assumptions. The second kind of seeing is the exact opposite of such probing and prying: it is a letting go, a waiting, a receptivity, an acceptance of the gift of the moment. In this kind of seeing, the mind must still and the words cease in order for the eye simply to *gaze* and receive whatever may be given in the moment of seeing. 'When I see this way I stand transfixed and emptied', says Dillard.

As we learn to look in these different ways, we may start to see things differently. We notice what we might have passed by as ordinary or of no consequence. We recognise what is going on underneath the surface. With William Blake, we may 'see a World in a Grain of Sand/and Heaven in a Wild Flower'. We start to 'see Jesus' in new ways, new places, new faces. We see him where we might not have expected him to be. And we see him *as* we may not have expected to: not only as the familiar healer, Saviour, Lord and crucified one but also as baby, as boy, as girl-child; as African, Indian and Aborigine; as angry as well as mild; as enigma as well as answer; as joker as well as solemn teacher; and in countless other guises.

And as we begin to see Jesus in new places and new ways, something more may happen. We not only *see* Christ, we begin to *encounter* him. The seeing becomes a two-way exchange. Perhaps you know that lovely story about the old French peasant who sits in the village church, day after day, for hours at a time, apparently doing nothing, not even praying. When the priest can curb his curiosity (or suspicion?) no longer and asks the old man what he is doing, the peasant replies: 'I look at him, he looks at me, and we are happy together'. As we seek to look with deep attention at Christ in the Bible, in the vision of artists and in the experience of people of faith very different from us, we may find Christ looking at us, gazing out at us from the painting or from the Bible text or from someone else's words or experience – challenging us, probing us, sifting us, taking us deeper into ourselves and into places where God wants to lead us.

The learning process

The approach to adult learning taken in this study guide emphasises learning as a *process of open exploration, enquiry and mutual discovery*. There is a given content offered for exploration, to be sure, but the real learning takes place when the material here is taken and used by those who actively engage with it. No 'right' or 'wrong' answers are assumed, but avenues for exploration are offered in the conviction that all truth is of God and that God is present wherever enquirers earnestly seek truth. Each person coming to the material will bring their own life experience, faith story, insights and questions which can illuminate the material and bring it to life in numerous ways.

The role of the group leader, when the material

is used in a group setting, is to be a support for the explorers in the group. The function of leadership can be shared around the group, a different person taking the leadership each time, or it can be invested in one particular person. However leadership is exercised, the leader is also a learner, perhaps with a little more experience or formal education than others in the group, but essentially a learner too. The leader is not expected to provide the 'answers' to the group's queries, but to structure each session so that all may learn. The leader therefore needs to create a 'safe space', so that each person feels comfortable and at home, free to participate as they are able, knowing that their contribution will be respected and accepted. Time taken at the beginning of the group to build up trust and confidence will be time richly repaid. The leader needs to encourage in each group member sensitivity to other people in the group. It is important to allow space in a group for individuals to make their own reactions and responses to the pictures, and not to judge any reaction as 'right' or 'wrong'. Working with powerful images can open up deep feelings and memories, and it may be helpful to alert group members to this at the beginning of each session.

How to use the material

Each of the 6 studies that follow consists of two main sections, as well as the picture itself and suggested biblical texts. First, a *learning process* is suggested for each group meeting, with suggestions for gathering, ways of looking at the picture, how to explore and unpack the picture and how to relate it to the Bible and our lives; suggested questions for sharing and for bringing the session to a close in prayer are offered, as well as a final sending out. The basic learning process should be manageable within a group meeting of one and a half to two hours, if carefully planned and the time well kept. For groups with more time, an additional activity is suggested, which could form the basis of a second meeting (making ten sessions in all) or could extend the session to a study day.

Accompanying the suggestions for the learning process are the *background notes*, which are chiefly intended for the group leader but may also be shared with the other participants, perhaps by extracts being read out or summarised by the leader. These notes provide information about the picture and the artist, the cultural setting and background to the work of art, as well as some brief notes on the relevant Bible passage(s). They are not to be used slavishly or to be seen as providing definitive 'answers', but to be drawn on as a resource as appropriate to the group. The notes on the biblical text are brief, since the main focus is on the artist's response to the biblical story or text. Groups wishing for fuller notes on the biblical texts might find it helpful to consult biblical commentaries.

The pictures are reproduced as A3-sized posters. It is vital that each member of the group can see the picture clearly. Ideally, each group member could have their own copy of this book. Where this is not practicable, the poster should be detached from the book and clearly displayed in full view of all. It may be helpful if the picture is passed around the group so that everyone has a chance to look at it more closely, in good detail. Sitting around a table with the picture in the middle may be a good way of ensuring that everyone can see the picture clearly.

However leadership is exercised in the group, each group session will need careful preparation. The practical resources listed at the beginning of each study will need gathering together, the room prepared, and decisions taken about the timing of the session and exactly which parts of the process are to be included.

Resources for further study

All that you need to follow the course of study, either individually or as a group, is provided in this guide. However, those wishing to pursue ideas arising from the material further may find the following resources helpful.

Sr Wendy Beckett, *The Story of Painting: The Essential Guide to the History of Western Art* (Dorling Kindersley, 1994)
Sr Wendy Beckett, *Art and the Sacred* (Rider, 1992)
Hilary Brand & Adrienne Chaplin, *Art and Soul: Signposts for Christians in the Arts* (Solway, 1999)
Richard Harries, *Art and the Beauty of God: A Christian Understanding* (Mowbray, 1993)
Edward Robinson, *Icons of the Present* (SCM, 1993)

SESSION ONE

SEEING JESUS AS A BABY

Aim

To ponder the wonder of Jesus born into the ordinariness of life, and to consider our response to the gift of Christ.

Picture

'Manger and gift bringers', by Lorraine Calaora, Philippines

Bible texts

Matthew 2:1-12; Luke 2:8-20

Resources

Bibles. For extra optional activity: materials for collage

LEARNING PROCESS

Gathering

Take time to gather as a group. You may like to open with a brief prayer, asking the Holy Spirit to direct your sharing and seeing. The following prayer can be used:

Come, Holy Spirit:
give us eyes to see and ears to hear,
minds to enquire and hearts to quicken.
Enlarge our thinking,
inspire our speaking,
enliven our praying
and deepen our living.
For we ask it in the name of Jesus Christ.

Since this is your first meeting, take time for each person to introduce themselves and say one thing they are hoping to learn or gain from your time of study over the coming weeks. It may be appropriate to share initial thoughts and feelings about studying the Bible through art. Do individuals feel excited or daunted by this?

Looking

Now focus on the A3 poster of the picture for this session. Make sure it is displayed so that all members of the group can see it clearly. Take at least 2 or 3 minutes to look in silence. Then invite people to share in pairs what they notice in this first gaze. Remember, there are no 'right' or 'wrong' responses. Accept in a spirit of openness what each person sees and offers.

Exploring

Now focus in more detail on the picture, using the following questions and background notes as appropriate (not to provide 'answers' but to stimulate further reflection) to guide discussion.

- What kind of world is the nativity set in? How does this compare and contrast with the biblical world into which Jesus was born?
- How many kinds of life can you see in the picture? How are the different people, animals and contexts responding to the

baby Jesus in their midst?

- What contrasts do you notice in the picture?
- What is the centre or focus of the picture?
- How is the manger itself portrayed? What meaning do you see in this?
- What is going on between Mary, Joseph and Jesus? What does this tell you about the meaning of Christ's birth?
- What are the individuals bringing to the manger?
- What words would you use to describe the image as a whole?
- What feelings does it evoke?
- How do you respond to it?

Sharing

Now read the two biblical texts, slowly and thoughtfully. Take a short time in silence after each reading to ponder the new insights into the passages provided by the picture.

Invite people to share in pairs one or two key insights they have found in the picture, and how this relates to their own life and situation. Individuals could be asked to consider the question, 'Where do I see myself in this picture?' (This is intended as a more focused, personal sharing than the wider ranging discussion above.) As an alternative to the activity below, these insights could be shared in the wider group.

Optional activity

Using a large roll of old wallpaper or several large flipchart sheets stuck together, make a group collage or painting of the nativity, setting the scene in your own neighbourhood and including individuals and scenes from your own local, regional and national life. Place yourselves within the picture (this can be done by using photographs of group members or by each person drawing an image of themselves).

Summary

Spend 5 minutes reflecting in silence on the question, 'What have we seen of Jesus?' Invite people to share one brief phrase or sentence summarising a new insight.

Closing prayer

Jesus, you are born into the midst of life as one of us.
You are not protected from the tensions and troubles of the world:
the extremes of wealth and poverty,
the contradictions between city and country,
the tensions between human greed and the needs of creation.
Yet as a helpless baby you become gift to us,
showing us how to create love in the midst of poverty and injustice,
joy in the midst of struggle and need.
So gift us with the ability to recognise you in our midst
and generously to offer ourselves in love to one another and to your creation
that we may help to bring to birth more of your divine life in our world.

Sending out

Go out from the group with a renewed intention to look for signs of Christ's love and joy in the midst of contradiction and the bustle of life this coming week. You might like to keep a journal during the week, keeping notes of how your reflection on the picture and texts develops as the days unfold.

BACKGROUND NOTES

The picture

'This is brilliant. The artist has got all the story of Christmas happening in the Philippines today. I think that's the meaning of the incarnation. But it's no kind of sentimental Christmas card. It seems authentic to me to have the poor bringing their gifts, while the Magi fly in. It makes me think about what it would be like if Jesus was born in my town this Christmas.' (Paul)

This picture was commissioned from the Philippines for an advent calendar made by four British charities. **The artist**, Lorraine Calaora, a popular illustrator of children's books, **sets the nativity in her own native Philippines**, and uses wonderful local colour to bring the scene alive. There is an immense amount of detail in the picture, bursting into and off the edges of the frame – almost as if there is too much life to cram into one picture; it cannot be contained but spills over beyond the artificial edges of our two-dimensional image. The more one looks, the more one sees, and it is worth taking time to keep on looking in order to glean all the richness and variety of life that Calaora depicts.

It is a picture brimful of *life* in all its colour, manifold dimensions and contrasts. **There is a wealth and diversity of *human* life**: people working in the fields and travelling on the roads; anonymous people whom we cannot see but know are present in the buildings, ships, vehicles and aeroplane as well as the particular individuals lining up with their gifts for the infant Jesus – and of course the three individuals at the centre of the picture, Mary, Joseph and Jesus himself, who radiate simplicity and humanity. But human life is only one dimension of the life in this picture. The artist depicts also a **wealth of *animal* and *natural* life**. The animals in the foreground – the ox, turtle, cat, pig, hen and cockerel, as well as the donkey disappearing off the lower right-hand edge of the frame – are each depicted with loving detail and care, and seem to possess as much individuality and character as do the humans. And **creation itself is present in a diversity of forms:** the verdant green, steeply stepped hillsides, the woods and plunging valleys, the cultivated fields, the tranquil ocean and starry skies (which seem to combine both daytime and night-time light) and the islands in the distance, all are vibrant with colour and growth. But it is not simply a rural idyll: the painting includes city life in the distance, with its high-rise buildings, commerce and wealth and busy harbour. All of life is here, colourful and teeming in its extraordinary ordinariness. Christ is born into this scene of bustling, ordinary life, one of earth's creatures, sharing not only the human life of the ordinary people of this picture, but also the life of the animals and the earth itself. **Christ is born in and *for* all of created life**, the picture seems to say, **one of us and sharing both the richness and the perplexity of created life.**

At the centre of this bustling, everyday life stands the manger, lifted up high on a kind of platform and standing out from all that surrounds it. In contrast to the ordinariness and even poverty of much of the rest of the scene, the stable is depicted in highly stylised form, rather like a Buddhist temple, richly decorated with sculptured forms and strewn with opulent gold woven rugs. The dominant colours are gold and red, suggesting wealth and majesty. The Christ-child

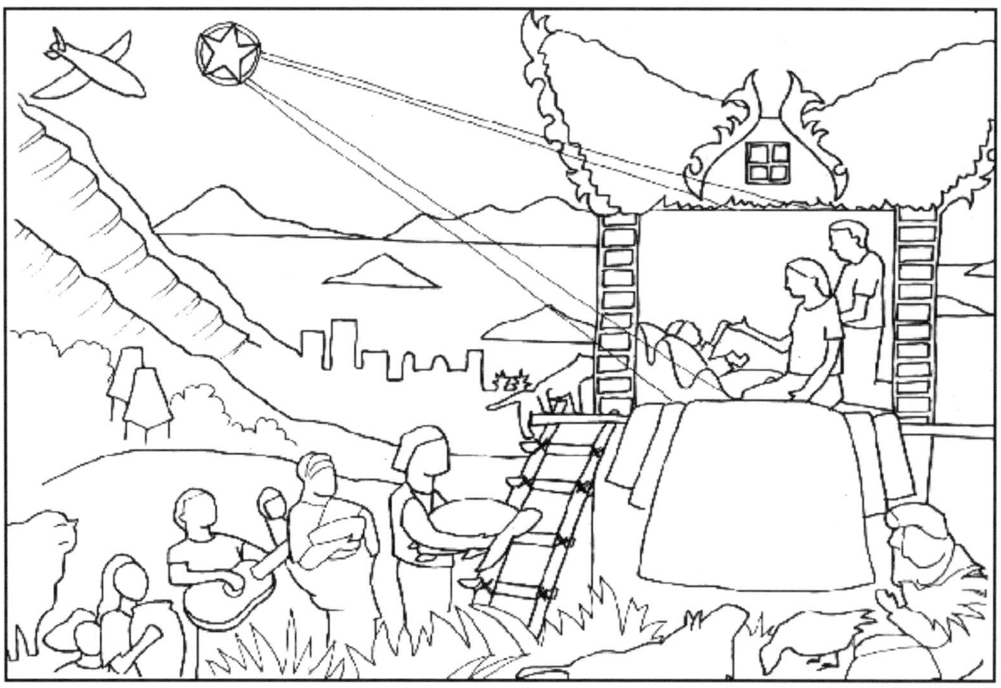

himself lies in an enormous shell, symbol of birth and baptism, as well as pilgrimage, and great waves of creamy gold light emanate from the baby. **Something of immense significance and sacredness is clearly present here, at the heart of the painting.** Yet within the richly decorated and plush frame of the stable, there is an immense stillness and simplicity in the relationship depicted between the three characters, the mother, the father and the baby. The child reaches out a hand to grasp the mother's finger in a gesture that is common across the world, and the mother and father gaze back down to the child in wonder and love. There is a sense of this family being utterly rapt in love, completely unselfconscious and absorbed in the giving and receiving of love that passes from one to the other. In their giving and receiving of love, they radiate a light to all around of which they seem entirely unconscious. **It is as if they are the mirror of the divine life within the Trinity, a life of perfect love and harmony which, with the birth of Christ, now becomes tangible and visible upon earth**, available to all who will see it and share this life.

Many in the picture do seem to recognise and respond to the marvel that is unfolding before their eyes. A great procession of human and animal life is making its way to the manger, to share in the love and the joy that is radiating from it, and to offer what gifts they can in homage and thanksgiving. The animals appear to have got there first, the pig looking on in rapt wonder and attention! But the humans are not far behind – simple peasants and ordinary folk, like the shepherds of Luke's narrative, bringing the gifts of their livelihood: animals and pottery and woven textiles, as well as gifts of music and praise and their own adoration. Notice it is the simple, ordinary folk who come (but not all – some are still in the fields working), recognising the Christ in their midst, whilst the rich and wealthy are too busy making money in the city or out on the seas on their luxury cruise liner! Or perhaps the Magi are jetting their way in on the aeroplane that is approaching? **The artist leaves us guessing, but there seems to be something powerful being stated here about the rich and the poor and how it is the poor who get to the manger first.**

Is it an idealised painting? Perhaps. All is verdant, green and harmonious, nothing seems out of balance. There are no mosquitos or mess in the manger. No one in the line approaching the stable looks tired or hungry. It is an image of creation and incarnation that wants to celebrate the fullness of God's life in the world, inviting the viewer to awe and wonder and praise – almost as if we are being invited to join that queue up to the stable to offer our gifts, whatever they are. Yet it is not a painting that ignores potential disruption, conflict or social struggle. The contrasts between wealth and poverty, city and countryside, human and natural world, are all there in vivid technicolour, and if the artist depicts these different dimensions of life in balance and harmony, it is not because such harmony already exists but because, in Christ, all of creation is *intended* to live in mutual interdependence and balance. **The picture challenges us to consider how we contribute towards such a vision of cosmic harmony or, in contrast, constitute part of the problem.** Thus it is an image that raises questions for the viewer, as well as offering a vision of hope towards which we are invited to work. And there are hints of the potential cost of such redemption, both for God and for humanity. Look again at the stable and notice references to the cross present in the window over the crib and in the two ladders at the side. Even here, in this wonderfully joyous, vibrant scene, suffering and death are foreshadowed. All of those who recognise and respond to Christ in their midst will find themselves drawn to the cross, as well as to the joy of nativity.

The Bible texts

The biblical texts accompanying this picture are the well-known ones of Matthew's account of the visit of the Magi to the stable, and Luke's story of the shepherds. They are often conflated in Christmas retellings of the story, and perhaps the artist has drawn on both of them here. But her sympathies seem to lie more with Luke than with Matthew. In Matthew's story, the emphasis is on fulfilment of Old Testament scripture (see Matthew 2:6) and the recognition of Christ by strangers 'from the east' (2:1) (presaging the drawing of the Gentiles to Jesus) who travel far in search of the newborn king or messiah (a key Matthean title for Jesus). In Luke's account, it is humble shepherds out in the fields with their sheep, preoccupied with nothing more weighty than their everyday duties, who are astounded by the angels' message and drawn to the crib. They are 'terrified' (Luke 2:9), but the angel assures them that the news of Jesus' birth is *good* news which will bring 'great joy for the whole nation' (2:10). In Lorraine Calaora's scene, it is the humble peasants going about their ordinary business who recognise and respond to the Christ-child in their midst, rather than any wealthy visiting dignitaries.

SESSION TWO

SEEING JESUS AS A BOY

Aim

To ponder the mystery of Christ made known in and through many different faith traditions and cultures.

Picture

'The boy Jesus in the Temple', by Frank Wesley, India

Bible text

Luke 2:41-52

Resources

Bibles. For the optional extra activity: symbols from a variety of world religions (for example: a menorah or a skull cap, a turban or other of the five symbols of Sikhism, a copy of the Qur'an, a picture of one of the Hindu deities) brought by members of the group, or provided by the group leader.

LEARNING PROCESS

Gathering

Open with a brief time of prayer, using the prayer from week 1 if preferred. Share briefly any insights or ideas that have emerged during the week. What have members of the group noticed while going about their daily life? Have you paid more attention to visual art in the media and in the streets, for example? What has stayed with you from last week's session?

Looking

Now focus on the A3 poster of the picture for this session. Take at least 2 or 3 minutes to look in silence. Then invite people in pairs to share what they notice in this first gaze.

Exploring

Focus in more detail on the picture, using the following questions and the background notes as appropriate to guide discussion.

- What kind of context is the scene set in?
- What different symbols and images are used? What do they suggest or convey? How far do you recognise the symbols and relate to them?
- How are colour and style used by the artist? How do you respond to both elements?
- How is perspective employed in the picture? What is the effect of framing the incident at a distance from the viewer?

- Pay attention to the three main scenes in the centre of the picture. What is happening in each? How do they relate to each other and to the outer frame?
- How would you describe the depiction of Christ in this scene?
- What does the image convey to you about where Christ is to be found in our contemporary world?

Sharing

Now read the suggested biblical text, slowly and thoughtfully. Take a short time in silence to ponder the passage. Share initial reactions to the incident, around two key questions: 'How do we see Jesus in this story?' and 'Where do I see myself in this story?'

Optional activity

As a group, spend some time looking, handling and speaking about the various symbols of different world faiths that members of the group have brought with them. Ensure that this is done with respect, making sure that scriptures are not placed on the floor or under other books, for example, but also allowing individuals to ask questions and articulate their own curiosity. The focus should be on 'seeing Christ' within the different faiths, and sharing in a positive way the contributions made by each of the different faiths to our understanding of God.

Summary

Spend 5 minutes reflecting in silence on the question, 'What have we seen of Jesus?' Invite people to share one brief phrase or sentence summarising a new insight.

Closing prayer

Christ, you are the source of all wisdom
and knowledge,
and all truth comes from you.
Open our eyes to see you in different
cultures, faiths and traditions,
and to receive the questions and
challenges you put to us.
Reveal yourself to us as guide and guru,
manifest in many different guises.
Expand our limited sight of you,
and teach us to recognise you in new
ways and new places
as we go out from here this week.

Sending out

Go out from the group with a renewed intention to look for Christ's presence and God's truth in different cultures, traditions and faiths this coming week. Keep notes about this, being honest about where you find this hard – or even impossible.

BACKGROUND NOTES

The picture

'I'm intrigued by the multicultural images, reminiscent of Mughal architecture. To me it says Jesus is for all humanity. There's Buddhist symbolism of enlightenment, a menorah from Judaism, space for women and black people. I love the delicate tracery and the subtle, vivid colours.' (Anon)

This picture is one of many by Indian artist Frank Wesley which depict biblical scenes within the cultural and religious traditions of 20th century India. Born in 1923, Wesley comes from one of the oldest Christian families in North India and from a long line of musicians and artists. His work is famous in his native India, and has been exhibited around the world. Influenced by the Lucknow watercolour and Bengal renaissance traditions of painting, his technique involves a layered transparent watercolour style requiring great time, patience and technical skill. Through this style his paintings achieve a glazed effect and a glow as if from within the canvas, which can have as many as 30 layers of paint.

We see the results of this technique in Wesley's depiction of the story of Jesus teaching the elders in the temple. It is a highly stylised rendition of the story, immaculately realised, with great precision and attention to detail. It is reminiscent of a medieval miniature with its large, elaborately decorated margins, its rich, jewel-like colours, and its complex religious and cultural symbolism. The border design and the design on Mary's cloak are distinctively Rajasthani. (Rajasthan is the second largest state in India, situated in the north-west of the country, with its own distinctive culture and history.) The architecture has a Mogul (or Mughal) Islamic style. (The Mogul empire was founded by Babur in 1526 and was a powerful dynasty which had a deep impact on the art and culture of India.) The niche in which Jesus sits could be a Mihrab, the place in the mosque where the person leading prayer sits, indicating the direction in which Muslims pray and generally considered the most sacred place in the mosque. All of this would be deeply familiar to Wesley's Indian contemporaries.

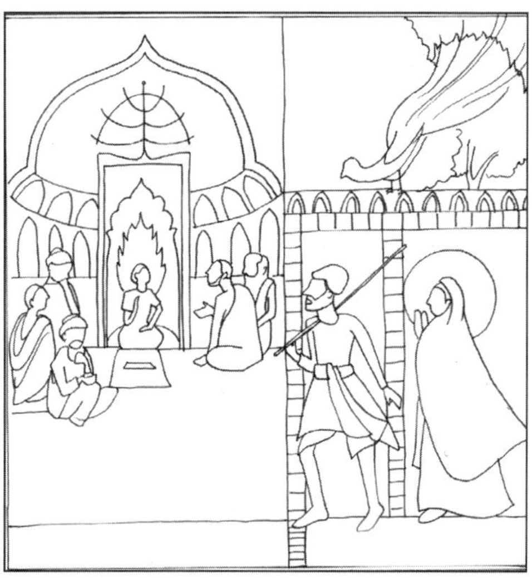

Within the framed scene at the centre of the painting, Christ sits surrounded by holy men from various religious traditions (one can detect a Buddhist monk, a Hindu yogi and a Confucian), teaching them from the scriptures. He sits slightly apart from them, and at some distance from the viewer, emphasising his uniqueness and authority. He is seated in the posture of one who would chant the scriptures in a Sikh gurdwara, the holy text carefully placed in front of him on richly decorated cloths. A golden flaming fire emanates from his head, fire being the symbol in all religious traditions of transformation and renewal of life, denoting spiritual power and force, transcendence and illumination. Above the Mihrab is the menorah, the seven-branched candlestick of Judaism denoting the divine presence. **Everything bespeaks Christ's holy and transcendent status, his great wisdom and authority**, and the holy men around him listen avidly, though also engaging in dialogue with him.

Just above this scene, to the right, and occupying a significant proportion of the picture, we see an image of the peacock against a mass of green foliage. The eyes of the peacock's tail feathers symbolise the hundred eyes of all-seeing divinity, but Frank Wesley intends it primarily as a sign of the glory of Christ. The great bushes of green seem to suggest fecundity and life, a symbol perhaps of the paradisial life that Christ brings.

In contrast to the somewhat static image of Christ teaching in the temple, the lower right-hand section of the inner frame is full of movement. Joseph and Mary hasten towards the temple in search of their son. Joseph's staff and Mary's cloak spill out of their portion of the picture, breaking the straight lines that everywhere else contain the action of the painting. Notice that Joseph is depicted as dark-skinned and black-bearded, whilst Mary is much fairer of skin, ivory-coloured. This is a cross-cultural marriage, emphasising once again the cultural and religious diversity at the heart of Christ's human life. And this is surely the central focus of the painting. **Christ is depicted as a guru and holy man utterly at home within the diverse religious traditions of our modern world.** He converses with representatives of all faiths, and is knowledgeable about each of them. There is no conflict between the different traditions and ways. Christ is lord of all of them, and formed by each of them. **Wherever men and women of faith seek God with sincerity of heart and humble openness**, the picture seems to say, **they will encounter Christ in their midst**, teaching and instructing them.

This insight challenges western Christians very deeply, since we have been accustomed to thinking of Christianity as set against other religious traditions, representing the only way to God. Like Mary and Joseph who have lost their Jesus and do not know where to find him, there may be a sense of 'losing' the distinctiveness of Christian faith if we risk true encounter and dialogue with people from faiths and traditions very different from our own. Yet, as the story and the painting suggest, Joseph and Mary's anxiety was misplaced – and ours may be also. They were operating at the human rather than the transcendent level, and had to discover that their boy Jesus was already well ahead of them in wisdom and understanding, and was embarked upon a way that they could only respect but not fully follow. **Perhaps we too have to discover that Christ is ahead of us and already making himself known in places we have feared to enter, recognised and welcomed by foreigners and strangers who may be nearer to God than we suppose.**

How do we respond to this painting? It is highly stylised and the image of Christ is perhaps an idealised and rather remote one. There is no doubt or conflict in this portrayal of Christ. He is very sure of himself, his identity and his calling. It is the transcendence of Christ that is emphasised here rather than his humanity. Perhaps we may find ourselves responding rather more warmly to Joseph and Mary's very human concern to find their son. Whatever our response to the painting, there is much here for us to ponder and pray over.

The Bible text

The biblical story is the only one in all four gospels concerning the childhood of Jesus, which otherwise remains closed and mysterious to us. This story therefore gives us a tiny glimpse into the formation of Jesus as a child and his relationship both to his parents and to the religious culture and authorities of his day. The story emphasises the devout adherence of Jesus' family to the law as they fulfil the obligation of annual pilgrimage to Jerusalem for the Passover. His parents do not understand Jesus' larger vocation to attend to his Father's business, are anxious when they cannot find him and 'astonished' to find him in the Temple. Nevertheless they are devout Jews who are bringing up their son in the knowledge of the scriptures and in the traditions of the faith – and this is surely part of the source of his 'wisdom' and 'intelligence' (verses 47, 52), though not the whole of it.

It is significant that the event takes place in the Temple. Luke begins his gospel with Zechariah serving in the Temple (1:8ff) and ends it with the disciples praising God in the Temple (24:52-53) at Jerusalem. Jerusalem is a key focus for Luke, signifying the heart of Jewish tradition, where the gospel must be preached before spreading out to the 'farthest corners of the earth' (Acts 1:8). Even in childhood, Jesus is shown as one deeply rooted in this Jewish faith, able to converse and dialogue with its teachers, addressing and being addressed by the scriptures. Another underlying theme in the story is Jesus' journey to Jerusalem, which is a key image for Luke, expressing Jesus' obedience to the will of the Father which will take him to Jerusalem and ultimately to the cross (see Luke 9:51).

The heart of the story comes in verse 49, where Jesus expresses an extraordinary conviction about himself, his identity and his destiny. The phrase 'Did you not know *I was bound* to be in my Father's house?' (REB) translates the Greek word 'dei' which is found often in Luke/Acts and expresses a strong sense of compulsion and divine necessity. Even from childhood, Jesus has a profound sense of his calling and is obedient to the divine mission, over and above his obedience to his earthly parents. Yet still he submits to their authority (verse 51), and continues to be formed by their love, care and discipline, growing in wisdom and favour, both human and divine.

This story therefore expresses something of the way in which **Jesus was formed within the riches as well as the limitations of a specific time, culture and religious tradition, submitting himself to those ways in order to know how to address and challenge his people's understanding and traditions**. Wherever the gospel is lived out, there is this tension between being rooted in the culture and traditions of a particular place and time, and challenging and questioning the limitations of any given cultural setting with the universality of the gospel. Frank Wesley's image of Luke's story helps us to think about the way in which the gospel has taken root in many different places and traditions, and can still speak both challenge and truth in many different settings.

SESSION THREE

SEEING JESUS AT A WEDDING

Aim
To reflect on and experience something of the abundant life that Christ brings.

Picture
'The Wedding at Cana', from the Mafa Life of Jesus series, Cameroon

Bible text
John 2:1-11

Resources
Bibles. For the optional extra activity: a meeting room large enough to enact a 'tableau' of the Bible story; large water jugs/bottles; wine or grape juice; other symbols of festivity brought by the group (for example, brightly coloured cloths, something good to eat, best clothes).

LEARNING PROCESS

Gathering
Open with a brief time of prayer, using the prayer from week 1 if preferred. Share briefly any key insights or ideas which have emerged during the week. Where have you encountered, seen or heard people of different faiths? What did you learn from the encounter(s)?

Looking
Now focus on the A3 poster of the picture for this session. Take at least 2 or 3 minutes to look in silence. Then invite people in pairs or in the whole group to share what they notice in this first gaze.

Exploring
Focus in more detail on the picture, using the following questions and background notes as appropriate to guide discussion.

- What kind of context is the scene set in?
- How would you describe the mood and 'feel' of the picture?
- How are colour and style used by the artist? How do you respond to both elements?
- Pay attention to the detail of the scene: the bride and groom under the canopy at the back, surrounded by musicians; those in the foreground drinking and talking; Jesus and his mother by the

water pots; the children; the villagers going about their business in the background.

- What do you notice about the way the artist has depicted Jesus and Mary – the placing of these characters in the scene, the colours of their clothes, the gestures they are using? How do you respond to the image of Christ?

Sharing

Now read the biblical text, slowly and thoughtfully. Take a short time in silence to ponder the passage. Share initial reactions to the incident, around two key questions: 'How do we see Jesus in this story?' and 'Where do I see myself in this story?'

Optional activity

As a group, create a 'tableau' of the biblical story set in your own context and culture and using the symbols and props you have brought. Choose people to play the parts of Jesus, Mary, the bride and groom, the servants and guests at the wedding. Share some food and wine and reflect on what it would mean for Jesus to turn water into wine in your life, your church, your community. Take it in turns to step outside the scene and comment on what you see. If you have a skilled artist in the group, you could ask them to do a quick sketch of the tableau – or get one member of the group to take a photograph to bring back next time.

Summary

Spend 5 minutes reflecting in silence on the question, 'What have we seen of Jesus?' Invite people to share one brief phrase or sentence summarising a new insight.

Closing prayer

Christ, you are the One who turns our poverty to plenty,
you are the One who pours the wine of celebration into our lives –
the finest of wines, choicest of choice.
May we welcome you into the midst of all our feastings and rejoicings,
and risk the fullness of life you promise to those who follow you.
Help us to share your overflowing flagons of wine
with all who are thirsty, all who are joyless.

Sending out

Go out from the group with a renewed intention to look for Christ at work in all places of rejoicing and celebration – and to bring Christ's joy into places of sadness and deprivation.

BACKGROUND NOTES

The picture

'I didn't spot that this was a miracle of water into wine at first. It looks like a village scene, but the big bloke on the left has just discovered something exciting in the jar. Jesus is a tall African, with his back to the artist, in red. I guess this is more like a traditional wedding in Jesus' time than a British wedding today would have been.' (Julie)

This picture is one of a larger series, the 'Mafa Life of Jesus' project, emerging from the small village of Mafa in the north-eastern hills of Cameroon in Western Africa and produced for teaching and preaching purposes. The artist, a French woman (whose name, interestingly, does not appear on any of the associated literature), lived and travelled in the villages, telling stories of Jesus, and asking people, 'How would this story have been if it had happened in your village?' Villagers created tableaux in response to this request, from which the artist produced sketches and paintings. This project has now been in existence for some 25 years, and more than 60 scenes have been produced. These are sent all over the world in the form of posters, cards, and recently on video and on the net. As a correspondent from Cameroon says, 'The images speak to people here, they understand right away the sense of the scene which is placed in a familiar surrounding.' (Further information and examples of other paintings can be found at www.jesusmafa.com)

What is familiar to the rural peoples of Africa may well seem foreign and remote to British viewers. Yet the freshness of these scenes set in a very different geography, climate and cultural milieu from our own can help us to see and experience familiar Bible stories in new ways. We don't need to know anything about the African cultural setting to recognise the joy and life in this village scene. **There is a great sense of bustling, joyful activity happening in every part of the picture.** We see villagers revelling in the wedding celebrations: in animated conversation in the foreground, in music-making at the back of the picture where the bride and groom are seated in the positions of honour, and in drinking from the gourds. And it is not only adults who are participating in this happy scene: children and animals have their place too, as in the first scene we explored, the Philippine nativity. We, too, as onlookers, are drawn into the scene: several characters look straight out at us, beckoning us in, as if we too are being invited to join this merry throng. **The artist conveys life and joy through the use of colour, as well as in the bodies and gestures of her characters.** Not only are there the rich, splendid colours of the wedding party's clothes, but the whole picture is suffused in a glowing, golden light, which is particularly intense in the left-hand corner of the painting where the water jars stand. This gorgeous golden light is reminiscent of liquid gold and of the amber colour of a deep, rich, fortified wine. It expresses something of the rich life that Jesus brings, and that this miracle signifies.

Yet, in other ways, the scene is wonderfully downbeat. As the quotation from Julie above suggests, we can look at this scene and regard it as 'just' an ordinary African village gathering, especially if we do not already know that it is the depiction of a biblical scene. **Jesus and Mary could be any African mother and son**, and the picture is subtly rather than blatantly focused on them.

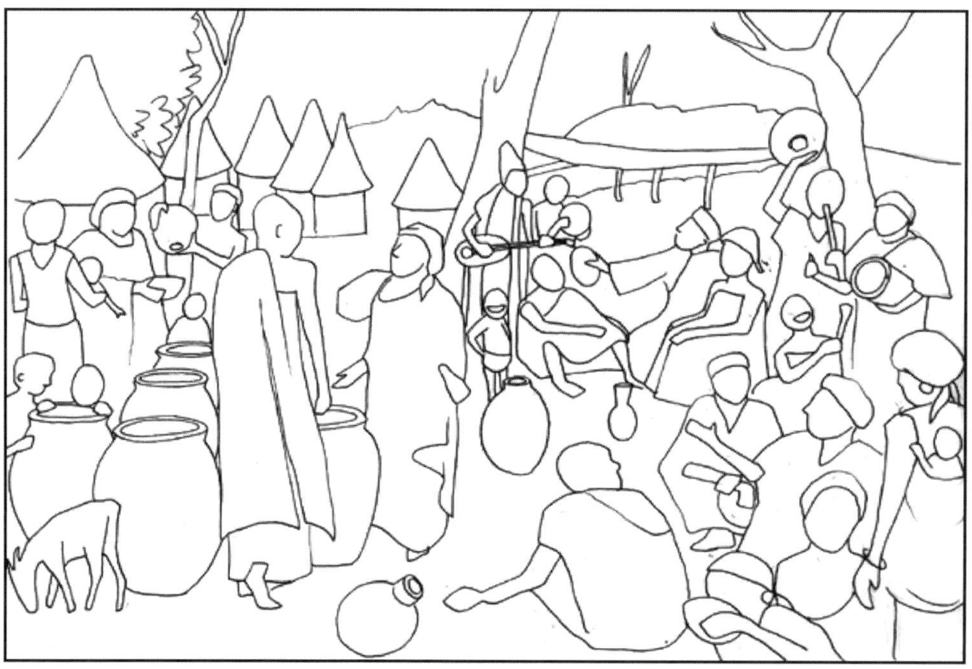

Jesus, in particular, remains enigmatic. In a stroke of genius, the artist paints him with his back to us so that we do not see his face – thus focusing on his action in transforming the wedding and the community that is gathered here, rather than on his identity as such. All we can see of him is his dark, muscular, young body and his gorgeous red robe – symbolising regal majesty but also the suffering of spilt blood. We see much more of Mary, robed in blue (a colour of status in Cameroon) and gesturing towards Jesus, open-handed and open-faced as she confronts Jesus with the lack of wine. We do not see how Jesus responds, yet there is a quiet intensity about this encounter between mother and son that suggests something of deep significance is happening here. **There is a focused stillness in this part of the painting, which contrasts sharply with the busy hustle and noise of the surrounding characters.**

The painting also downplays the miracle. It is not immediately apparent that there *is* any miracle here. It is interesting to speculate on the precise moment in the story that is being depicted. Is it just before the miracle takes place or is this the very moment when the water is miraculously transformed into wine? The face of the large, gold-attired man on the left of the painting perhaps suggests the latter – his face is a picture of amazed delight as the drops of wine are poured into his bowl. But perhaps it is a look of consternation as he realises the pot is empty and there is no more wine left for his guests? The artist does not make it obvious, and we are left guessing. **Perhaps the real miracle is not so much in the transformation of the water into wine as in the joy and abundant life that are evident in the whole scene** – and it is this the artist wants us to focus on, rather than on the miracle itself.

How do we respond to this painting? Its charming simplicity and character of rural idyll is immensely appealing and, in contrast to the previous image of Jesus in the Temple, where the viewer was kept at a distance, we are drawn into this scene and brought very near. Yet for most of us in Britain who live in large urban conglomerations, the picture may remain rather remote and unreal. Nevertheless, even if this is not *our* ordinariness, it *is* ordinariness – a bustling village scene in which Jesus is completely at home, and to which he contributes his life and his capacity to create abundant joy. It can therefore help us to think about the ordinariness of our lives and the invitation of the gospel to invite Christ into the centre of our ordinary lives to make and multiply joy.

The Bible text

This biblical story (which is unique to John's gospel) is the first of Jesus' 'signs' or miracles in John, in which Jesus manifests his 'glory', revealing himself as Christ (Messiah) and saviour. Typical of the gospel as a whole, this story is full of rich symbolism, particularly messianic symbolism, reflecting theologically on who Jesus is and what a right understanding of him is. **The wedding banquet is a traditional symbol of the messianic age when the Messiah will come, and wine is a sign of gladness, joy, hope and promise** (see Isaiah 54:4-8; 62:4-5) as well as of the *eschaton*, the end time when history will be consummated (see Amos 9:13; Hosea 2:21; Joel 3:18; Isaiah 29:18; Jeremiah 31:5-6). Jesus' action of transforming the water in the jars used for the rites of purification is a symbol of his transformation of the old rites of Judaism into something new. The cleansing of the Temple follows this incident – another event showing Jesus' authority and status as Messiah. John wants to leave his readers in no doubt of the identity of Jesus.

The place of Mary in this story is also of interest: it is one of only two places in John's gospel where she appears, yet she acts as catalyst and mediator, bringing the lack of wine to Jesus' attention and directing the servants to do what Jesus tells her. In this, she acts as a true disciple, indeed, as the foremost disciple in the new community of the church. John emphasises her role as a disciple, rather than as an individual or even as the mother of Jesus, as is indicated in his calling her 'Woman' rather than mother in verse 4. His apparently harsh response to Mary here needs to be read in the light of John's high Christology (that is, an understanding of Christ which places a strong emphasis on his divinity) and heightened emphasis on Jesus' freedom and transcendence.

In contrast to the synoptic gospels, Jesus in John knows his identity and his destiny from the beginning, and is fully in control of all that will happen to him. Not even his mother can shape what he is to do or hurry the 'hour' which will surely come when he will accomplish what he has been sent to do (namely, offer his life upon the cross). **This first miracle, then, which is one of great joy and abundance, nevertheless points forwards to Jesus' last and greatest 'sign': the sign of the cross, in which he will effect the transformation of human life and community** which we see here taking place in microcosm, in a village wedding where Jesus is the guest.

SESSION FOUR

SEEING JESUS AT A DISTANCE

Aim

To reflect on the challenge of faith in difficult times when Jesus appears to be distant or absent.

Picture

'The Centurion's Servant', by Stanley Spencer, United Kingdom

Bible text

Luke 7:2-10

Resources

Bibles. For optional extra activity: materials for creative writing: paper, pencils or pens, a dictionary and thesaurus.

LEARNING PROCESS

Gathering

Open with a brief time of prayer. Share any key insights or ideas which have emerged during the week. Where was joy and celebration present during the week? Were there any further thoughts on any of the previous weeks' stories or pictures?

Looking

Now focus on the A3 poster of the picture for this session. Take at least 2 or 3 minutes to look in silence. Then invite people in pairs or in the whole group to share what they notice in this first gaze.

Exploring

Focus in more detail on the picture, using the following questions and background notes as appropriate to guide discussion.

- What is happening in this picture?
- Who are the characters? What are they thinking, feeling and doing?
- How would you describe the mood and 'feel' of the picture?
- How are colour, light and shade used by the artist? How do you respond to these elements?
- What do you notice about the setting of the scene? How do you interpret it?

- Where is Jesus in this painting?
- Where is faith?
- What kind of healing is longed for or needed here? Is it purely physical healing, or something else? Something more?

Sharing

Now read the biblical text, slowly and thoughtfully. Take a short time in silence to ponder the passage. Share initial reactions to the incident, around two key questions: 'How do we see Jesus in this story?' and 'Where do I see myself in this story?'

Optional activity

Invite each member of the group to identify with one of the three characters around the bed or with the sick child in the bed. In the persona of that character, write a prayer to Christ, expressing your thoughts, feelings and the needs for healing that you see. Alternatively, rather than writing down your prayer, work in pairs and talk about the kinds of things you would want to say to Jesus.

Summary

Give members of the group the opportunity to share what they have written or said (but no one should be compelled to do so). Spend 5 minutes reflecting in silence on the question, 'What have we seen of Jesus?'

Closing prayer

Christ our healer,
you are present to us in shadow and darkness,
in sickness and in need,
even when you appear to be distant and our prayers unanswered.
Help us to trust you in our waiting and to have faith like the centurion,
so that your healing may be released into our homes and our communities,
and your saving power made known in our world.

Sending out

Go out from the group with a commitment to pray for some person or situation that needs healing (interpreted in its widest sense), and to pray for one another that your faith may be strengthened and renewed.

BACKGROUND NOTES

The picture

'This could be any house in England a hundred years ago, where sickness or death caused sorrow and agony. The title tells you that this is a picture about waiting for Jesus to do something. That's a common experience for Christians like me, so to me the picture is all about prayer. God wins in this story, but the waiting and the praying are part of the story. At the end, the servant is made well.' (Andrea)

This painting is one of many by Stanley Spencer in which gospel stories and scenes are transposed to his native village, Cookham, in Sussex, and in which people he knew from the village appear as the characters. Spencer (1891–1959), widely regarded as one of the 20th century's most significant British painters, was brought up in the Christian faith and steeped in the literature of the Bible and Christian classics such as the writings of Bunyan and Milton. Although as an adult he developed his own somewhat unorthodox beliefs, he continued reading the Bible until his death. His overriding concern was to unite the sacred and the profane which he saw as unnecessarily separated and treated as opposites in much religion of his day. He regarded painting as 'spiritual work' or 'religious activity', bringing him closer to God.

This picture was painted by Spencer in 1914, when he was just 21. It is marked by an intensity of vision and a certain innocence, apparent here in the depiction of a childhood scene, although in other ways the painting seems far from naïve. Spencer himself appears in the scene as the central character: the boy on the bed is Spencer as a child, and the boy looking on appears to be another version of Spencer. The room is the servant's attic room at Fernlea, where Spencer was born and spent much of his life and where, as a child, he heard voices and imagined it was the maid talking to an angel. **The painting fuses such childhood memories, including the memories of people praying around the bedside of a sick person, with the Bible story, and with Spencer's own faith struggles.**

It is a mysterious, even a disturbing image. Although it is based at least in part on the gospel story in Luke, the mood and feel of the painting are very different from the emphasis of the biblical text. In Luke's story, the emphasis is on the faith of the centurion and the subsequent healing of the servant. In Spencer's version, the dominant mood seems to be one of anxiety, foreboding and anguish, and there is little, if any, sign of the longed-for healing. **It is a troubling painting, one that raises many questions rather than offering answers.** Its historical setting at the start of the First World War perhaps helps to explain something of the dark foreboding which is apparent; Spencer himself was wrestling with the decision whether to enlist for service or not and the consequences this would have for himself and his art. The painting therefore comes out of a very real struggle with questions of morality, faith and art, and, as yet, the struggle seems to remain unresolved. The artist did finally join the Royal Army Medical Corps and served initially at a hospital in Bristol, caring for injured soldiers from the Western Front, before being sent in 1916 as part of the 68th Field Ambulance unit to Salonika. His Burghclere Memorial Chapel paintings of 1926–1932 record many scenes from this time, depicting the sufferings of the soldiers with a simple and profound compassion.

Our painting shows a deceptively simple scene. The vast bed dominates the centre of the bare room and, whilst it is an utterly particular, real bed – with specific features, the wrought iron, the red valance, the blankets and covers – it also seems to function as an existential symbol of human mortality. **Bed is the place of human conception, birth, sleep, illness and ultimately death, and so as a symbol, it encapsulates the whole of the human journey from birth to death.** The power of the symbol is intensified by the stark,

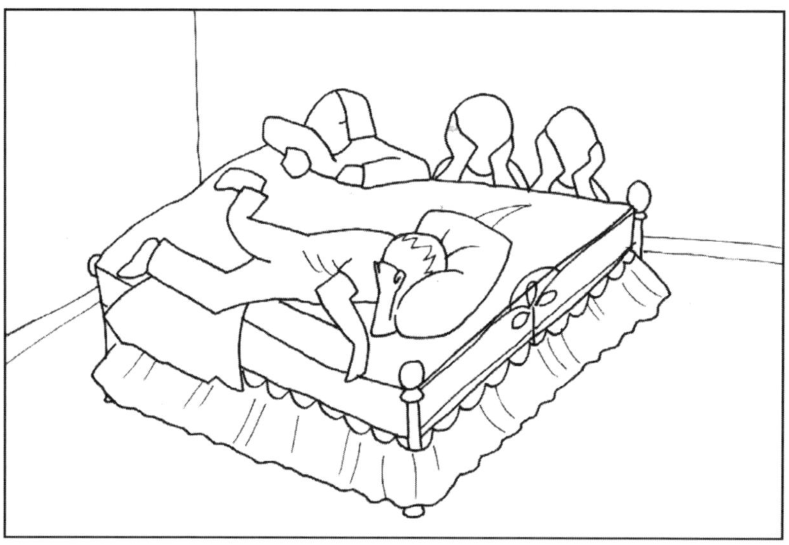

bare surroundings. The detail and the colour of the bed contrast dramatically with the great empty space of the room in which it is set, with its bare floorboards and shadowy black wall. A window is suggested but it lets in no light and through it we can see nothing. It is as if the bed floats, suspended, in a great sea of darkness and shadow, suggesting the loneliness and hazard of the human journey through life.

This sense of impending hazard and loneliness is communicated by the four characters, too. The boy on the bed lies contorted, with his face averted from the three who kneel on the other side. He has one hand covering his mouth and, with the other one, grasps the edge of the bed. It is difficult to interpret the look on his face: is it pain or boredom? He appears utterly isolated, unaware of the presence of the three who look on, in various gestures of anguish and supplication. These three themselves show no signs of connection with one another; each is enclosed in their own private world of grief and struggle. Spencer calls attention to the hands as much as the faces of his characters: one has clenched knuckles raised to her face, the second rests his head in his hands in a gesture of despair or resignation, and the third throws out his (or is it her?) elbows and twists his head in writhing anguish. There is immense movement here, but the movement somehow does not suggest development in the story. **All the characters appear held, trapped within their situation of sickness or despair, and there is little sign of help or healing at hand** – unless it is in the turned head of the child on the far end of the bed, looking for or hearing the approach of the returning centurion?

Where is Jesus in this painting? Conspicuous by his absence! In many ways, **this painting conjures a yearning for divine presence and a powerful sense of divine absence which is in striking contrast with the other more confident images we have been considering** which boldly assert Christ's presence in the world, real and tangible and close. Yet, in its own way, Spencer's troubling image may be as powerful for us as any of the other images. For us, as for Spencer and the people in the painting, Christ may well be the one longed for and yearned towards rather than the one confidently known and grasped; the one waiting for us in the darkness and the shadows, beyond our conscious knowing or comprehension: one who is perpetually mysterious and in whom we may well feel uncertain, unsure of our own belief. This Jesus is one whose presence we pray for and towards, in anguish and despair, when we are desperate for our own or for others' healing, when we long for a word or a sign to resolve our moral uncertainty and spiritual struggle. Does he come? Spencer's painting seems to remain ambivalent; and **this is an honest portrayal of longing faith that remains uncertain of itself, suspended in shadow**. Yet this is how it may be for us who struggle with faith – at times or indeed, for some, most of the time.

The Bible text

In Luke's gospel, the biblical story of the healing of the centurion's servant (which appears also in Matthew and John), forms part of a larger section (7:1 – 9:6) which is concerned with the way in which Jesus crosses over conventional religious boundaries separating clean and unclean. Gentiles, tax collectors, sinners and the profoundly sick are shown as those who hear Jesus' word and respond to it, in contrast to those who might have been expected to do so, but do not. So in this story, the centurion, a Gentile army officer, shows great faith. The Jewish elders commend him to Jesus because of all that he has done for the nation, but, in contrast, the centurion himself proclaims that he is not worthy to have Jesus under his roof. Had Jesus come to his house, he would have broken the rules of ritual purity; the centurion does not want to compromise Jesus by putting him in this situation. However, Jesus finds him worthy because of his great faith, and heals his servant from a distance, commending the example of his faith to all those present.

This story of a centurion's faith has a strong parallel in Acts 10, where another centurion, Cornelius, cares for God's people by almsgiving and is a man of great faith and prayer (Acts 10:1-2). He is used by God to show Peter that God makes no distinction between Jew and Gentile, but looks for faith and responds to such faith by bestowing salvation (or, in the Greek meaning of the word, healing).

These two stories in Luke and Acts, alongside Spencer's painting, raise profound questions about the nature of true faith. They perhaps suggest rather different answers. In Luke/Acts, faith is clear and certain, confident in the saving power of Jesus Christ to heal, redeem and renew lives and communities, whereas in Spencer's painting, faith appears much more anguished and opaque. **Taken together, however, the painting and the biblical text can address each other in challenging ways and provoke contemporary believers to think again about what lies at the core of our faith.**

SESSION FIVE

SEEING JESUS IN ANGUISH

Aim

To contemplate the suffering of Jesus and pray for people and places of suffering in our world today.

Picture

'Crown of Thorns', Anonymous, Africa

Bible texts

John 19:1-3; Isaiah 53

Resources

Bibles. A selection of pieces of wood and/or sculpture – rough and smooth, different kinds of wood, different colourings and markings, etc. For optional extra activity: a selection of recent newspapers, writing materials.

LEARNING PROCESS

Gathering

Open with a brief time of prayer. Share any key insights or ideas which have emerged during the week. Where and how did Jesus seem distant or absent? Where was there a need for healing? Where were people waiting and crying out for Christ?

Looking

Now focus on the A3 poster of the African sculpture. Take at least 2 or 3 minutes to look in silence. Then invite people in pairs or in the whole group to share what they notice in this first gaze.

Exploring

Focus in more detail on the picture, using the following questions and background notes as appropriate to guide discussion.

- What do you notice about the characteristics of the wood? How has the sculptor used the medium to create this powerful image?
- What would it be like to touch and handle this piece of sculpture? (It may be helpful to pass around various pieces of wood for members of the group to feel and comment on, as a way of helping the group to imagine what it would be like to handle the sculpture. Invite them to close their eyes and focus on the sense of touch as you pass the wood around the group.)
- What do you see as the dominant

characteristics of Jesus in this sculpture? What words would you use to describe his facial expression?

- Does the fact that the sculptor is unknown and anonymous affect the way you relate to the image?
- How does the image make you feel? What situations and people does it bring to mind?
- What does the Jesus of this sculpture say to you or ask of you?
- What biblical texts, passages or stories does this image call to mind for you?

Optional activity

Using a selection of recent newspapers, invite members of the group to find and cut out stories, pictures or items of news that depict contemporary suffering. Place these around the image of the sculpture. You might like to light a candle and place it alongside the cuttings and image of Christ. Use the cuttings and images as a focus for a time of silent prayer. Read the biblical texts slowly as a lead into the time of prayer. Individuals may like to take a verse from the Isaiah text and meditate upon it quietly during the time of prayer, or they may like to hold one of the pieces of wood as a tactile focus for their prayer. Before you begin, agree how long you will spend in prayer so that people do not become anxious about the time. 10-15 minutes is a suggested guide, but this may be too long for groups with little experience of silent prayer. End with reading the short passage from John 19.

Summary

Invite each person to take a sheet of paper and a pen and write down in one line or phrase a simple prayer addressed to the suffering Christ OR a sentence expressing what they think Jesus is saying in this image. Give members of the group the opportunity to share what they have written (but no one should be compelled to do so). Spend another 5 minutes reflecting together in the group on the question, 'What have we seen of Jesus?'

Closing prayer

Lord Jesus,
surely you have borne our griefs and
  carried our sorrows.
All the anguish of the ages is known to
  you;
you bear in your flesh the wounds and
  smarts of suffering.
Give us courage to gaze into your
  sorrowing face without flinching,
and not to turn away from your anguish
wherever we see it in the suffering flesh
  of our brothers and sisters,
both near to us and around the world.
Teach us the tenderness of your
  compassionate touch,
and show us how to carry the burdens
  we must bear.

Sending out

Go out from the group with a commitment to pray for some person or situation where suffering is deep and ongoing. Ask Christ to reveal himself in or to that person or situation.

BACKGROUND NOTES

The picture

'An African Jesus, so broken and sad you expect the wood to start weeping. Amazing how the sculptor has made the wood so spiritually expressive. There seems to me to be pain, but also acceptance in this work. One to sit with quietly and take in slowly. What a thing to produce from a block of wood!' (Jane)

This detail of an anonymous African sculpture, perhaps from Nigeria, is an extraordinarily powerful, affecting piece. The impact of the sculpture, presumably all the greater in the presence of the actual artwork, is nevertheless captured in this photograph, with its close-up focus on the face of Jesus and the subtle lighting which highlights the rich red and gold colours. We are enabled to see the detail in the grain of the wood and its natural blemishes, including the scar that runs down from the hair onto the forehead of Jesus, which the artist has not attempted to hide but rather has used to heighten the sense of physical and mental suffering.

Like all great sculptors, this anonymous artist seems to have looked deep into the original piece of wood and released its secret inner life, finding the perfect medium for his – or her – vision. He or she has worked *with* the flow and texture of the grain rather than against it, incorporating its unique characteristics into the finished image. As Anna, a secondary pupil, expressed it, 'The grain of wood runs with the feeling of the moment like tears'. Although this is just a photograph, it is so tactile and sensuous an image that we feel we can almost touch the wood. Our eyes caress the smooth wood of the forehead, nose, cheeks and lips; we can imagine our fingers running along the finely matted hair and feeling the sharp prick of the thorns, or picking out the intricate lines of the beard. **We are invited in very close to this image, to share in the deep suffering and anguish of the wounded Christ.** And of course it is not insignificant that the artist chooses wood as his or her medium – the very stuff out of which the cross itself was made. The wood that was used to crucify Christ is here redeemed by being formed into a thing of immense meaning and beauty. The ugliness and shame of the cross are transformed into beauty and honour.

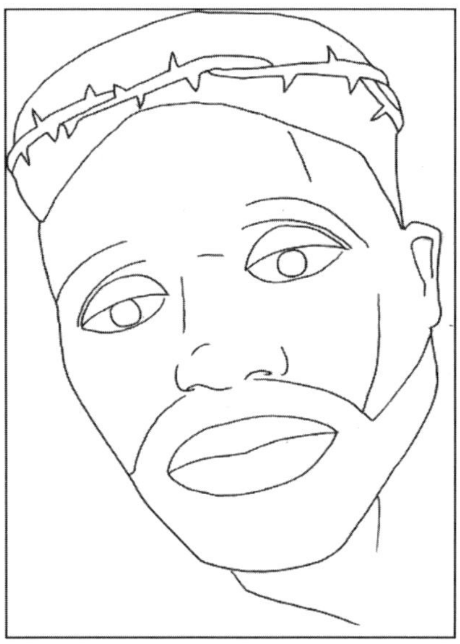

There is both anguish and dignity in this African image of Christ, as if he bears sorrows of which we, the onlookers, remain unaware. He has the bearing of someone regal yet also utterly humane and simple – as of a king incognito, a ruler who lives among his people and shares their poverty and plight. He is an African, burnt by the sun; we might say he is *the* African, representing the anguish and suffering of an entire continent and people. This representative character of Jesus is emphasised all the more because the sculptor remains anonymous. This is typical of much non-western, non-European art, which is communal in emphasis, coming out of an entire people's experience and insight rather than being the product of one person. The artist may be the one who translates the experience and vision of a people into tangible reality, but in this he or she is only a medium, a servant. The important thing is the shared experience out of which a particular insight or achievement comes – and this is not something 'owned' by any one person, but shared by all.

So it is with this African Christ. **He is not a mere historical individual, but a representative, the representative human one and, in the depths of his suffering and compassion, he shows us God and so is also God's representative on earth.** He seems to carry and express the depths of African humanity and the suffering of centuries in his visage and expression. Centuries of European colonisation; the abuse, humiliation and injustice of slavery; the appalling effects of racism; the suffering of natural disasters; poverty, disease and malnutrition; the devastation upon families and communities of Aids and the HIV virus – all these forms of anguish and more are borne by Christ. And borne with a dignity and a kind of mute acceptance or resignation that makes us think of the Suffering Servant. This Christ does not cry out against the injustice of suffering or rail against God and humanity; like the Suffering Servant, this Christ bears the suffering that is laid upon him, bears it and absorbs it and somehow takes it into himself, his very body and being, and there lets it find rest. We are given here an immensely moving image of divine compassion and redemption in the form of Christ the sacrificial victim who offers himself on our behalf to endure the suffering that he himself has not deserved. God, in the form of Christ, comes among us as one of us and, though without sin and undeserving of death, takes upon himself the weight of human sin and suffering and offers it to God for our healing and salvation.

Above all, it is the suffering, crucified Christ who has appealed to Africa over the centuries. **It is only such a Christ who can speak to the depths of African oppression, suffering and struggle.** This is well expressed by the South African poet, Gabriel Setiloane, in his long confessional poem, 'I am an African':

And yet for us it is when he is on the cross,
This Jesus of Nazareth, with holed hands
and open side, like a beast at a sacrifice;
When he is stripped naked like us,
Browned and sweating water and blood in the
heat of the sun,
Yet silent,
That we cannot resist him.

How like us he is, this Jesus of Nazareth,
Beaten, tortured, spat upon, truncheoned,
Denied by his own, and chased like a thief in
the night,
Despised, and rejected like a dog that has fleas,
for NO REASON...

In the face of such suffering and such profound acceptance of suffering, we can only gaze and adore.

The Bible texts

The short extract from John describes the soldiers' weaving of a crown of thorns for Jesus as part of the mocking and humiliation of Christ. The other gospels describe similar scenes (Matthew 27:27-31; Mark 15:16-20; Luke 22:63-65; 23:11), though Luke does not mention the crown of thorns. John highlights Jesus' royalty by placing his mockery as king at the centre of his trial by the Romans.

The well-known passage from Isaiah 53 is one of the so-called Songs of the Suffering Servant, in which a beloved and chosen one suffers vicariously for the sins of the people and is redeemed by God. Much scholarly debate has been expended on the identity of the servant and various hypotheses put forward, but the most likely explanation is that the servant represents Israel or a remnant of faithful Israel. This, the fourth song, emphasises the suffering, humiliation and rejection of God's servant. The servant suffers in silence (verse 7), submitting himself to being pierced, wounded and crushed (verse 5), like a sacrificial lamb. The passage describes his arrest and sentencing, hinting at his death and burial (verses 8-9), yet speaks of the way in which God preserves the servant's life (verses 10ff). By his suffering, the servant 'justifies' many (verse 11) and through him, 'the Lord's purpose will prosper' (verse 10). Although the servant suffers now, victory will come and he will be delivered from all his sufferings. 'After his suffering he will see light and be satisfied' (verse 11).

Throughout Christian history, these servant songs have been applied to Jesus. Many have seen them as prophecies pointing forwards to the cross, and predicting in a detailed way the fate of Christ. Even if scholars today do not read them as such predictions, emphasising that they have an integrity within the context of exilic Judaism, they remain powerful and moving poems speaking of suffering as part of the destiny of God's chosen ones, and of the redemptive possibilities of suffering freely accepted. They can speak of the history and vocation of God's people Israel, and of the suffering of other peoples throughout history – including that of Africa – as well as of the history and suffering of individuals such as Christ and many who have followed in his footsteps subsequently, walking the way of humiliation, rejection and death. Nevertheless, **the Servant Songs remain enigmatic and mysterious confessions of faith – not only in the sense that the identity of the servant remains enigmatic, but in the sense that they raise many more questions than answers.** Why does God call some to suffering, and why is suffering necessary as part of the journey of faith? As Teresa of Avila put it in her acerbic fashion, if this is how God treats his friends, no wonder he has so few! How can one person or group suffer on behalf of others and how may such suffering be redemptive? Is all suffering potentially redemptive or is some suffering simply oppressive and destructive? These kinds of questions are not resolved by our texts or by the powerful image of the African Christ, nor can they be. Yet we may be challenged to think again about these age-old questions as we meditate on the biblical words and upon the image of the suffering Christ.

SESSION SIX

SEEING JESUS ON THE TUBE

Aim

To reflect on the presence of Jesus in ordinary, everyday life, and on our need to recognise him.

Picture

'Jesus on the Tube', by Antonia Rolls, United Kingdom

Bible text

Luke 24:13-53

Resources

Bibles. For the optional extra activity: Martyn Joseph song, 'One of us', on the CD 'Far From Silent' (50285 190198 2 0, 1999).

LEARNING PROCESS

Gathering

Open with a brief time of prayer. Share any key insights or ideas which have emerged during the week. Where was Jesus in anguish? Were you enabled to carry the suffering of others in some way? Did you see signs of redemptive suffering?

Looking

Now focus on the A3 poster of the picture for this session. Take at least 2 or 3 minutes to look in silence. Then invite people in pairs or in the whole group to share what they notice in this first gaze.

Exploring

Focus in more detail on the picture, using the following questions and the background notes as appropriate, to guide discussion.

- What is happening in this picture?
- Reflect on the setting. If you have travelled on the underground or metro, share your experiences. How is it different from, or similar to, travelling in a car, a bus or an overground train?
- Who are the characters depicted? What are they thinking, feeling and doing?
- How is Jesus depicted? What do you notice about his clothing, posture, gaze

and positioning in the picture?
- How do you respond to this painting? Do you find it comic, poignant, surprising, hopeful? Something else?
- What biblical texts, stories or themes does this painting call to mind for you?
- What do you see as the key challenge of this painting?

Sharing

Now read the suggested biblical text, slowly and thoughtfully. Take a short time in silence to ponder the passage. Share initial reactions to the incident, around these questions: 'How do we see Jesus in this story?', 'Where do I see myself in this story?', and 'What does the story tell us about seeing or recognising Jesus in our midst?'

Optional extra activity

Role-play the scene in the picture, taking it in turns to be the character of Jesus and the other characters (you can add in more). Find as many different ways of ignoring Jesus as possible. The character of Jesus can try actively to meet the gaze of the other characters, without talking. Afterwards debrief what it felt like to be Jesus and the other characters. Listen to the Martyn Joseph song, 'One of us'.

Summary

Invite each person to spend 5 minutes in silence reflecting on the question, 'How and why do I ignore Jesus?' Offer an opportunity for each person to share their response to this question, without comment or further discussion.

Closing Prayer

Christ of the everyday and the unexpected,
you are with us and around us wherever we go:
in the stranger sitting next to us on the tube,
in the old man wrapped up in his troubles
and the young executive busy with her affairs;
in the girl on the mobile phone
and the out-of-work young man hanging around the bus shelter.
Give us eyes to notice you in the stranger
and the willingness to encounter you in our neighbour.
Pierce our defences so that we may meet you
and greet you where you wait for us,
just around the corner,
at the next stop.

Sending out

Go out from the group with a commitment to keep your eyes open on the bus, the tube or the train; to take the risk of smiling at strangers and expecting to meet Christ in the people you encounter.

BACKGROUND NOTES

The picture

'Jesus fits into every aspect of society. He's with us always but leaves us with the choice to acknowledge him. We can choose to ignore him, but it will never change the fact that he is there by our side. Jesus is the only figure looking at you in this painting. He is always going to be interested in you because he wants to be our 'way out'. He'll wait patiently until we come to take that escape route.' (Emma)

This picture is by the contemporary, London-based artist Antonia Rolls, who brings a spiritual perspective to her work and paints with humour, colour and panache. Born in 1960, Antonia had a strong sense as a child of being an artist, though it took her many years to fulfil this vocation. After graduating from university, she worked for an economic consultancy firm in London, prior to marrying and having children. Her marriage ended in divorce, and this was the catalyst for her to decide she must prioritise her art in order to become a self-employed artist. In the early years, she had very little confidence and was at times so poor she could not afford to buy even a pint of milk. However, she persevered and gradually established a reputation, resulting in commissions abroad as well as in the UK, and many exhibitions. She says, 'The spiritual side to my life runs through all I do especially my work. I was brought up Catholic, went wider and explored Christianity then went off beyond that and started to look at what happens beyond the rules of religion.' She sees love as God's greatest and most liberating gift, and suggests that **'spiritual understanding does not only happen to other people but is open to everyone in the business of daily life'**.

'Jesus on the tube' provokes an immediate reaction. It has a surprising freshness and humour about it, as we contemplate Jesus travelling on the underground at Knightsbridge station. Anyone who has ever travelled on the tube will instantly recognise the cold, silent anonymity of the other passengers. **They are all engrossed in their own affairs and show blank or snooty faces, turned in upon themselves.** The business man in his pin-striped suit hides behind his newspaper, turning his face as far away from Jesus as he can – though he does not actually appear to be reading the paper. The woman next to him seems slightly anxious, with her raised eyebrows; she places her handbag on her lap protectively, as if to form some kind of defensive barrier, and she puts out her hand on the seat to keep a safe distance from the man sitting next to her. They do not touch; it is as if they do not exist to each other. The young woman sitting on the other side of Jesus appears to be half asleep, eyes cast downward, her body enclosed upon itself.

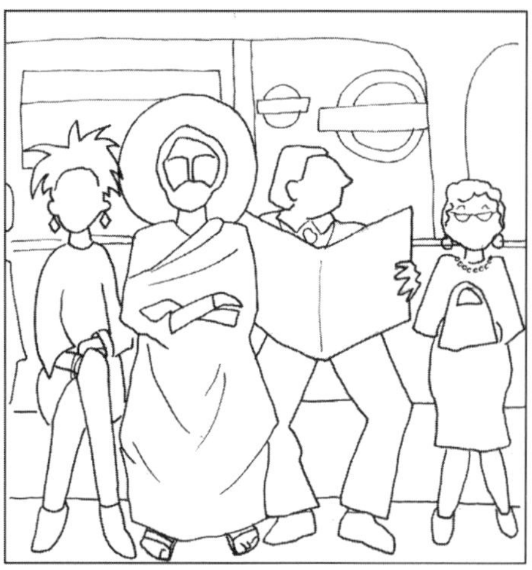

The context is interesting: a dark, enclosed space under the ground where the trains hurtle from one station to the next and the air is heavy and hot. Perhaps more than any other context of travel, this is a space in which people can feel in potential danger, trapped and vulnerable to the presence of people they do not know and do not trust. In rush hour the tube is packed and travellers squash into the carriages like sardines packed into a tin. Late at night the tube can feel a dangerous, uncomfortable place, especially for vulnerable people travelling alone. In such a space, people do not look at each other for fear of attracting attention to themselves or in case they open themselves to someone who may be mad, bad or needy. **It is a highly depersonalised space, in which distrust, self-protection and even hostility to others appear to be the order of the day.**

But the artist has not simply painted the underground in a general, abstract way. It is a specific station, Knightsbridge – one of the 'poshest', richest neighbourhoods in central London, and Sloane Street is a byword for 'yuppie-dom', the haunt of young, urban professional types. The characters reflect this setting. They are all white, they are impeccably dressed, they have an air of wealth about them. Perhaps the artist is suggesting that wealth and class contribute to the tendency to isolate oneself from others. **Those who are comfortably off may have less sense of their need of others, and may have more to defend.** We are reminded of Jesus' hard words about wealth: 'It is easier for a camel to pass through the eye of a needle than for a rich person to enter the kingdom of God' (Matthew 19:24).

What of Jesus himself? He is depicted in a vibrant red and yellow robe with a large gold halo, arms folded and feet solidly planted on the floor. In some ways he appears in the style of a traditional orthodox icon, and he stands out in striking contrast to the 'ordinary' contemporary dress of the other passengers. Yet in other ways **he appears *more* alive, *more* present and alert than any of the other characters present**. He alone gazes directly out at the viewer, seeming to compel a reaction from us, the onlookers. His folded arms seem to suggest 'I'm here to stay; what are you going to do about it?' His positioning in the painting is interesting. He does not seem to sit on the seat on the same plane as the other passengers. He is positioned slightly forward of the other characters, nearer to the viewer, almost hovering in the foreground. We feel we could reach out and touch him, so close to us is he. And then there is that sign above his head, 'Way out', calling to mind Jesus' saying in John, 'I am the way, the truth and the life' (John 14:6) and suggesting that Jesus represents a way out of the alienation, loneliness and isolation of the tube. Looking closer, we can detect a series of small gold dots all around the body of Jesus, setting him apart from the rest of the picture – almost as if he is a cardboard figure who can be cut out of the painting. Indeed, the other figures seem to have cut him out, frozen him out by their total disregard of him, their deliberate refusal to meet his gaze, to acknowledge his presence. Here we might be reminded of the Suffering Servant of Isaiah 53, who was despised and 'shunned by us all' (verse 3), humiliated and put to shame.

Is it a hopeful or a despondent image? On the one hand, it seems to suggest that Jesus is there in our everyday world, right close to us, ready to meet us on the tube, on the bus, in the queue at the supermarket. We do not have to search far for him, he is very near to us. He is one of us, sharing our space and our concerns. As Martyn Joseph expresses it in the song 'One of us':

What if God was one of us
just a slob like one of us
just a stranger on the bus trying to make his way home?

Just trying to make his way home, back up to heaven all alone,
Nobody calling on the phone,
'cept for the Pope maybe in Rome.

But the image, rather like the song, is not entirely hopeful. The painting seems to suggest that Jesus is ignored, rejected and frozen out by the majority of contemporary British people who are too busy, too self-absorbed, too rich or too preoccupied to make room for a stranger like Jesus. And the song suggests that Jesus may also be lost, like us, 'trying to make his way back home'. **He needs our help as much as we need his.** Perhaps this is the key to the image: the mutual interdependence of Jesus and humanity. **We need Jesus but Jesus also needs us, he wants our attention, our gaze, our friendship.** God also gets lonely if he is continually ignored, sidelined and rejected.

The Bible text

The Emmaus story is perhaps one of the best loved of the resurrection appearances in the gospels. It is such a rich and dense story that we cannot consider it in its entirety here – any decent Bible commentary will provide fuller notes on this text. The main focus for our purposes is on the theme of recognition, which is a central one in the story. The disciples do not at first recognise Jesus. He is a 'stranger' who travels with them, accompanying them in their grief. Unlike the characters in our painting, they do not ignore Jesus. They are glad of his company in their sadness, but they do not recognise him for who he is. Their sadness, grief and failure to comprehend the events of his passion and death seem to have blinded them from recognising the identity of Jesus their master. He patiently interprets the scriptures to them and explains all that has happened, how it had all been part of God's design (verses 25-27). Yet it is only when they welcome him in to table with them, when they offer the stranger hospitality, that finally their eyes are opened and they do then recognise him. As he takes bread, blesses it, breaks it and shares it with them, the scales fall from their eyes and they know it is Jesus, and worship him in their midst.

As for them, so for us: **Jesus is the one who travels alongside us in our troubles and incomprehension, as well as in our joys.** Jesus is the one who questions us about our experience, asking us the meaning of our stories. But he does not only ask the question, he also travels with us as we struggle to find the meaning of our experience and enables us to find new meaning as we tell our stories to his listening presence. Jesus is the one who interprets the scriptures to us, connects the stories of our lives to the wider story of God's dealings with Israel and the world, and thus gives our lives a bigger, deeper meaning. Jesus is the one who sits with us and eats at table with us, sharing our hunger and our bread, breaking the loaf with us and pouring the wine for us. **Jesus is the one made known whenever we welcome the stranger to our table, whenever we extend the handshake of hospitality to persons encountered on the road, bus or tube.**

ACKNOWLEDGEMENTS, NOTES AND SOURCES

Introduction

Annie Dillard's discussion of seeing forms chapter 2 of her extraordinary autobiographical essay, *Pilgrim at Tinker Creek* (Picador, 1976), which won the Pulitzer prize for general non-fiction. William Blake's poem, 'Auguries of innocence', contains the famous stanza quoted here, and can be found in numerous anthologies and in the *Collected Poems* (Penguin, 1991).

Session One: Seeing Jesus as a Baby

'Manger and gift bringers': © Lorraine Calaora.
The quotation on page 10 by Paul is one of a number made by school children in response to the images in the *Picturing Jesus* pack (Christian Education, 2001). These and other comments on the pictures can be found in the accompanying guidebook by Lat Blaylock, and are used with his permission.

Session Two: Seeing Jesus as a Boy

'The Boy Jesus in the Temple': from the book *Frank Wesley: Exploring Faith with a Brush* by Naomi Wray, Pace Publishers NZ.
Further information about Frank Wesley, with photographs and examples of his paintings, can be found at www.onemindonevoice.org/mentors/frankwesley.html. Additional examples of his work can be found at www.lib.virginia.edu/area-studies/SouthAsia/Misc/Wesley/wes.html.
Individuals and groups wishing to develop further their study of Jesus as seen by world faiths could gain much from a study of *Celebrating Jesus: a multifaith appreciation*, a collection of texts about Jesus from a variety of world faiths edited by Daniel Faivre SG, Michael Barnes SJ, Tony McCaffry and Edgar Lange (published by Daniel Faivre and available from him at 2 Church Avenue, Southall, Middlesex UB2 4DH).

Session Three: Seeing Jesus at a Wedding

'The Wedding at Cana': All rights reserved, Vie de Jésus MAFA, 24 rue du Maréchal, Joffre, F-78000 Versailles, FRANCE www.jesusmafa.com
For further notes on the biblical passage, focusing in particular on Mary's role, see *Remembering Mary* Study Guide by Nicola Slee (Christian Education, 2000).

Session Four: Seeing Jesus at a Distance

'The Centurion's Servant': © Estate of Stanley Spencer 2005. All Rights Reserved, DACS (photo © Tate, London 2005). There are numerous collections of Stanley Spencer's art widely available in libraries and at art galleries. In addition, a number of websites provide information about his life and art, and examples of the paintings. See in particular www.stanleyspencer.org.uk and www.angelfire.com/ar/stanleyspencer. Both of these sites provide other links.

Session Five: Seeing Jesus in Anguish

'Crown of Thorns': reproduced from *The Faces of Jesus* by Frederick Buechner with photographs by Lee Boltin, published by Harper & Row, with permission from Stearn Publishers Ltd. 1989.
The poem, 'I am an African' by Gabriel Setiloane, is published in T Wieser (ed) *Salvation Today and Contemporary Experience* (WCC, 1972, pp.32-34).

Session Six: Seeing Jesus on the Tube

'Jesus on the Tube': © Antonia Rolls, reproduced with the permission of the artist.
The information about Antonia Rolls and the quotations come from private correspondence with the artist. The Martyn Joseph song, 'One of us', can be found on the CD 'Far From Silent' (50285 190198 2 0, 1999). Permission has been sought for the use of the lyrics.